I0485226

# Performance Reviews

# The bad, The Ugly, …
# The Alternative

ISBN-13:978-1496144157
ISBN-10:1496144155

# Also by Oswald R. Viva

Customizing VLSI IC Update: A User's Guide
to the ASIC Design Center.
Electronic Trends Publications.

It's Lonely At The Top
A Practical Guide To Becoming A Better
Leader Of Your Small Company
iUniverse, Inc.
ISBN-978-1-4620-4653-9
ISBN-978-1-4620-4655-3
ISBN-978-1-4620-4654-6

Fundamentals Of Job Interviewing For
Managers
Amazon.com
ISBN-13 978-148022960
ISBN-10 1480222968

Accountability In The Workplace
www.SkillBites.net

You Are The Owner, But Are You The Right
CEO?
www.SkillBites.net

Create A Culture Of Empowerment
www.SkillBites.net

Delegate To Succeed
www.SkillBites.net

Exit Strategy And Succession Planning
www.SkillBites.net

# Table of Contents

# PREFACE

In the last several years there has been a flood of articles and commentaries criticizing traditional employee reviews and even calling for their elimination all together. The reasons given are many but they really amount to the fact that performance reviews don't do much for the employee or for the company. These publications argue against employee performance reviews but offer very little as alternatives. At most they suggest better ways to do them or different but similar processes than in reality suffer from the same problems. In this book I propose a valid alternative that has many advantages related to benefits to the employee, the manager and the employer.

Management of an organization—small or large—requires measurement of performance of all employees throughout the organization. How this is done is critical to the performance of the organization (company, department or group) and primarily to the development and wellbeing of each employee. Traditional management tools (performance reviews) have many flaws and some alternatives are either not well understood, are unfair or are unproductive.

A valid alternative should be welcomed by all concerned. The alternative proposed here is a proven tool that represents a significant improvement over the other methods used. I am not proposing anything new or revolutionary; to the contrary, my proposal is to use an old system, but one that is not generally used for the purpose of performance reviews. I propose that using MBO and RBGO will eliminate the shortcomings of standard performance reviews.

MBO = Management By Objectives

RBGO= Reviews By Goals and Objectives

# PART I - Standard Performance Reviews

## Traditional method

Managers hate them, employees hate them, they add little or no value and in most cases they "don't work"; so why do we do them?  What purpose do they serve?  Should they be done once a year, or is it twice a year?  What happens if they don't get done?

I'm referring of course to traditional employee performance reviews.  The business world taught us to do formal performance "reviews" of employees on a fixed schedule, as a standard management requirement.  But why?  Does this practice make better employees?  Does it make better managers?  Does it guarantee excellence in performance?  Do they really work?

W. Edwards Deming, the quality guru, says about performance reviews that they are "one of the seven deadly deceases of organizations".

UCLA business professor Samuel Culbert says that "they are dishonest and fraudulent and just plain bad management". [1]

Studies show that 97.2% of U.S. companies and 91% of companies worldwide use performance appraisals.  Given their ubiquity, why do performance reviews have such a bad reputation?

## Definition

Wikipedia defines a performance review or appraisal as a "structured formal interaction between a subordinate and supervisor, that usually takes the form of a periodic interview (annual or semi-annual), in which the work performance of the subordinate is examined and discussed, with a view to identifying weaknesses and strengths as well as opportunities for improvement and skills development."

## History

Employee performance reviews can be traced to the 1930s when they were applied in a Western Electric factory as part of a study on the behavior of workers. It was determined that happiness of employees and their productivity were directly related to the social structure of the workplace. Other references peg the start of pperformance reviews as a distinct and formal management procedure used in the evaluation of employee performance, to the early forties.

Then, and in many places even now, reviews were done strictly to adjust employee's salaries. Sadly, employee development was not considered, but the responsibility of managers wasn't to just hire someone to do a job; they had to manage and mentor people, too.

The U.S. government institutionalized this in 1950 with the Performance Rating Act, which mandated annual reviews of federal employees. Later, laws were enacted to tie salaries and bonuses to these assessments. Since then, performance reviews have evolved to include evaluation of the behaviors, motivation, values of employees as well as plans for the development of the workforce individually and as teams.

One obvious problem is that most managers are not trained in areas such as behaviors and motivation, and without proper training they are not equipped to use them. In fact, wrongful use of these specialized disciplines can cause more harm than good.

## Why have performance reviews anyway?

Why do we do performance reviews and what are the objectives of the review? Is it to evaluate the organization (company or department) and eliminate the bottom performers and recognize the top players? Is it to determine compensation standards? Is it to develop individual plans for personal development? In many cases this is unclear and that's one reason why managers conduct the task of reviewing performance so poorly.

Why do performance reviews rank so low on our list of things we look forward to as managers and employees? If we assume that the basic purpose of employee evaluations is to build better-performing organizations, then this should be one of the most important things managers do, but if formal evaluations weren't a management requirement, would they be done anyway?

In the second paragraph of this publication I asked the question: "Do performance reviews really work"? Please allow me to answer that question right now … No, they don't really work and are mostly a big waste of time and effort and in many cases they work negatively by demoralizing employees.

Let me explain:

Employees only like "review time" because they equate it with salary increases, but they only like reviews that are complimentary and hate those that are less than the "best". Managers hate getting ready for them, completing the forms and, mostly, facing the employee with bad news.

The review meeting itself, between employee and manager, can be a difficult experience for both. If the employee is a good performer and thus the review is a flattering one, the intercourse is usually pleasant and friendly, but it can get adversary if the salary increase offered is below the expectations of the employee.

On the other hand, a less-than-great review can be a difficult incident for both manager and employee. Universally, nobody likes to hear that one is "below average" or worse. Our ego or self-esteem wouldn't allow us to accept being negatively compared to peers.

Managers exit the meetings either feeling sorry for the employee, or with the uncomfortable feeling of having created an enemy. The employee surely decides that the manager doesn't like him/her or—at the very least—that the review was completely unfair. Seldom these experiences result in a more motivated employee and a happy relationship between the parties.

A good performance review should give employees constructive, unbiased feedback on their work, but a bad one can demonstrate supervisor bias and undermine employee confidence and motivation.

Performance reviews are one of the most dreaded and despised elements of corporate life. Just mentioning that a performance review is due understandably strikes fear and alarm in employees everywhere. Their anguish is justified because performance reviews are too often done poorly and employees fear what bad news it will bring.

It's not as if managers like them either. The tough of preparing for a review of a non-performing employee and getting ready for what surely will be a confrontational meeting is depressing to say the least, and for all reviews, filling the required forms, presenting the results and even justifying the changes in compensation, take away from the "normal" work of the manager and is viewed as a waste of time, which in most cases it is.

"Albert Smith's performance review doesn't seem to be going too well."

Performance reviews have long received poor grades, even from those who conduct them. Nearly 60 percent of human-resources executives graded their own performance-management systems a C or below, according to a 2010 survey by Sibson Consulting Inc [2]. It also said that 73 percent claim that the top HR executive is the biggest champion of performance reviews, and this can place managers against the HR department.

Just 30 percent said the chief executive was the major proponent, yet the directives from the top are that performance reviews must be done and they must be done on time. And one academic review of more than 600 employee-feedback studies found that two-thirds of appraisals had zero or even negative effect on the employee or the company. Why then top management dictates their application?

Reviews are counter-productive; according to a study by A. Kluger and A.Denisi in The Psychological Bulletin [3], 30 percent of the 607 performance reviews they examined ended up in decreased employee performance.

The process generally is not objective. It's one person's opinion (the manager) about another person (the employee) at a point in time (usually for the previous 12 months). They force employees to focus on securing favoritism with the boss, not on doing their best for the company. Managers are human and as such it is practically impossible for them to eliminate issues that may cause some form of favoritism or discrimination.

It is a proven fact that most managers tend to favor employees that they hired over those who came from other sources. In some cases there is favoritism related to gender, background, education, or even personalities, and they are hard to dissipate.

There is another factor that comes into play, and that is the effort and ability of some people to ingratiate themselves with their managers and the manager's blindness (often on purpose) to recognize it. This compounds the problem of unfair reviews by causing animosity among coworkers.

From a team perspective, performance reviews can make or break the internal relationships existing in it. Poorly executed appraisals and unjustified differences in the appraisal or resulting compensation of individuals can cause a lot of unhappiness and stir up turmoil This in turn can lead to a fall back in productivity and work satisfaction.

Have you ever experienced a year end review in which you received a message that you didn't agree with? I did, and I can tell you it definitely negatively affects work and work relationships.

Many years ago while employed by a large semiconductor company managing a large department, I had the unfortunate experience of losing my immediate manager in an automobile accident. He and I had an excellent relation and together we had made significant contributions to the company. Until that time all my reviews had been excellent and I was always classified as a top performer. Upon his demise I reported to a top excutive of the company who, in practice, was removed from the activities of individual departments or sections of the company.

My yearly review "was due" soon after the change and of course it had to be done by my new immediate superior. Not knowing of my individual contributions and the contributions of the department I managed, he gave me a poor review stating that "the entire division had a poor performance and thus everybody in the division was deserving of a classification as a poor performer".

Of course I disagreed vehemently with this and I told him that if the division had performed poorly, then he should be classified as a poor performer, and not those who individually had performed optimally. Needless is to say it had a profound negative effect on my motivation and it caused much unhapiness in "my" department as everyone felt unappreciated. As a result I requested an immediate transfer to another division, which robbed his division of key contributions.

I have also seen another facet of a badly formated and conducted performance review. A group manager confided in me that he gave poor reviews because he had received a very poor one himself and thus he didn't want his employees to appear to be better than him. A good example of bad management and insecure personality in addition to a not-so-nice behavior.

**Some reasons for the bad reputation of performance reviews:**

- Perception that the pay adjustment has already been determined by management either as general guidelines or specifically for individuals, so the bosses come up with a review that fits the adjustment; a backwards process.
- Forms can be cumbersome and inefficient and thus the manager hates to comply with them and puts the process off as long as possible.
- The focus becomes about process rather than about improving performance and giving meaningful feedback to an employee.
- The determination of salary increases or bonuses isn't fair and is often arbitrary or done with favoritism.
- Employees have no insight into the matter and receive no clear explanation as the reason for the classification and/or salary adjustment, so they have no choice but to accept what their boss tells them and with no recourse to disagree.
- There is no follow up after the review about things discussed in the review and there are no action items to help the development of the employee.
- Reviews are generally scheduled once a year (sometimes twice a year), and for the rest of the year, there's no focus on attaining long-term goals. *See later about why this is a problem.*

The criteria used to decide acceptance of performance should be well understood and agreed to by the employee and the data that determines performance should be known by the employee beforehand. Qualitative measurements must be fairly and universally applied throughout the organization.

## Competing agendas

Wharton management professor Matthew Bidwell suggests that performance reviews tend to have competing goals: Employees are looking for frank, honest and helpful feedback, but they realize that review time is an opportunity to showcase their performance to the boss and make a case in order to get a pay raise.

On the other hand, the organizations aim is to reward performance and contribute to the development of employees in a fair process. Ideally these two fronts should not be in competition, but in practice they can be—and many times they are. What management may see as needs of an employee to improve, the employee may not see and instead perceives management as working to limit present rewards.

"Mainstream management is embedded in, and relies on a culture of domination and the performance review is the biggest hammer management has", writes UCLA Anderson School of Management professor Samuel Culbert[4]. Feedback shouldn't be like a report card, he says. My take is that report cards are OK if they truly represent what the performance was and if they are used to improve performance, not to penalize the performer. Hammers don't fix performances or attitudes; reasoning, coaching and support do, and if they cannot be fixed there are other tools to be used rather than retaliation or a show of domination.

As I said earlier I have seen managers give poor reviews to good performers because the department or team did not perform well, without taking in consideration the individual performer or circumstances affecting the performance. Is a team member to be judged as the team or individually? I say that it depends on various issues, but it is not an automatic thing. At the very least the employee should be judged for his/her contributions to the team, and if the team failed, how the employee's contributions (or lack of them) affected the failure.

Yes, there are exceptions, and these usually happen when the two sides reach an understanding of the root causes of the underperformance, and of the measures to be taken by both sides to correct it.

A recent article in *The Wall Street Journal* [4] discusses some of the problems with annual performance reviews and how a few companies are abandoning them. In the article, the author mentions that even HR professionals recognize the flaws in the system.

But the main reason I'm against traditional reviews is that, in general, they don't provide anything positive to the enterprise. Do employees get to be better performers as a result of reviews? Do they learn new skills from it? Does the company benefit from increased productivity? Does the manager become a better leader by this practice? While I can't give an unequivocal NO to all these questions, I can confidently claim that the benefits—if any—are very minimal.

Many supervisors use their own personal/professional agendas as standards to appraise performance of employees and they use as criteria at least in part, how well an individual meets the supervisor's agenda. Unfortunately this is part of human nature as we are partial to those who are perceived to be most like us. A manager who worked for me at a large company used this as measurement of performance because he believed that his "agenda" was best for everyone; so, how should I have judged him?

"Let's start with some good news. Your last performance review got 2 million views on YouTube!"

## Improving performance reviews

Performance reviews are supposed to determine and communicate what the employees have been doing well, what they have been doing poorly and what they can do to improve. But just listing these items will not provide the benefits that should be expected. What changes are needed and what must be done to achieve them is necessary to get those benefits.

Performance reviews rightly place a lot of importance on the quantifiable, but employees should also be judged on qualitative things and these are not necessarily tracked for the review. They are also harder to measure with specific numbers and thus, without regular observations and coaching from management, these qualities go without being measured. The converse is also true and therefore a problem. Some managers don't place enough importance on the quantifiable and measure more abstract concepts without real knowledge of how an employee performs in these areas.

Performance reviews should be primarily competency-based and directly related to the job the employee is supposed to do. The job description should be used as the guiding document for the employee's position using a quantifiable analysis to decide where the employee excels and where he needs improvement.

An honest and complete discussion on the goals to reach, how to reach them, what help will the employee need to achieve them and—mainly—what role will the manager and the company play to help the employee progress, should be included in an ideal review.

A good review starts with a good preparation. Reviewing what the employee has done for the entire period analyzing in as much detail as possible his/her contributions, success of projects in which he/she was involved, team participation, response to company or department demands, and all other expected aspects of performance.

Input from others should be solicited including from his/her coworkers, other supervisors and people who have reasons to know the work of the employee (*see later in this book about 360 degree reviews*). Compare present period with previous periods and note changes (both positive and negative).

## The review meeting

It is imperative for the manager reviewer to have the right attitude for the review. Being impartial and without pre-conceived ideas is required; negative feelings about things that happened in the past or personality conflicts should not enter into play, unless of course are directly related to the performance of the employee.

The manager must think positively before going into the meeting and look at it as an important part of the job and not as a burden to "get rid of" as quickly as possible. Similarly, the employee should have the right attitude being receptive to the feeback received and disregarding hard feelings towards the manager or the company. Of course, I know that this is easier to say than to put in practice ...

Actions directly follow people's thinking and viceversa. Being in command does not mean being dictatorial. Feeling uncertain or dominant will impact the tone of the conversation. It is crucial for both—manager and employee—to become aware of their feelings before trying to change or influence something. It helps to "break the ice" at the start of the meeting by talking about non-related subjects, have a cup of coffee or a soft drink and a friendly exchange of ideas.

Both reviewer and employee must be open and friendly and say what they need to say but always in a soft manner and never raising their voices. The manager must cover the positives and include the learning points expected and achieved, giving constructive feedback with examples. Both must listen to what the other has to say and must ensure clear communication both ways; did the emploee understand the communication clearly and did the manager understand the employee's points clearly too?

If there is a sense that there are differences of opinion or displeasure, they should be dissipated before breaking up the meeting. If the employee lives the room feeling frustrated or misunderstood, it will be much more difficult to connect ongoing.

After reviewing performance for the review period, the meeting should shift to future performance by discussing and setting expectations for the next period *(see "setting goals" later in the book and Appendix 1)*. Expectations should include employee development goals as well as employee participation in team activities. Furthermore, certain behavior characteristics such as attitude towards the work, the job, management, and the company should be included in the goals to be pursued. The more effective supervisors spent the bulk of their performance evaluation meeting time talking about the future.

"He gives his heart and soul to every annual performance review."

### Frequency of reviews

One of the biggest problems with reviews is the frequency in which they are given. Problems should be addressed when they arise and good accomplishments should be rewarded without waiting several months to do it. A lot can happen in a span of six or twelve months that can affect the performance, the reviews or the relationship between manager and employee.

Is the employee the same weak link that he/she was when the period started, or did he/she change so much as to demand two different reviews? Was there a management change within the period? Did the employee change jobs? Departments? Does the manager remember everything the employee did at the beginning of the period, or is he/she being judged only by recent accomplishments or lack of them?

Although in most cases it is customary to complete the dreaded performance review on an annual basis, this is not the best option. While—as you will see later—I prefer real-time feedback, I propose a quarterly or even monthly review system that will help keep employees on track constantly. If you're waiting until year end to let your workers know they aren't performing well, it's only going to hurt your team and company's overall success. Additionally, employees will be less than thrilled to find out at the end of the year that they've been doing something wrong for months.

In a sports team the coach doesn't wait until the end of a season to give his players feedback; he does it immediately after a play or after the game when the feedback is going to do the most good. With a quarterly or monthly review system, you're able to give more timely feedback that can be implemented immediately.

Meetings between employee and supervisor are beneficial, but the discussion should be a positive forward-looking agenda, not a nitpicking review of the past. "My boss's rule is that if you're hearing something for the first time in the annual review, he hasn't done his job right," says Emily Faye Abbott, an assistant district attorney in Knoxville, Tenn.

"If you wait a year to tell employees how they are doing, they are almost always surprised and unhappy if the results are not positive" says Peter Cappelli, head of Wharton's Center for Human Resources. "Humans are hard-wired to focus on the negative, so balanced feedback always leaves us concentrating on the bad parts of the reviews".

Although I admire the work that Jack Welch did as CEO of GE, I do not agree with some of his "teachings" regarding treatment of employees, particularly when we consider small businesses. For example, in "Winning" [5] in answer to the question "how long does it take to know if you've hired right?" he says that one should know "usually within a year, and certainly within two". This may work for GE but in a small business—and generally speaking in any company— you cannot "carry a mistake" for a year or two.

Performance in some jobs are more difficult to define than in others, and some people are more difficult to evaluate than others, so setting an arbitrary time to detect and correct mistakes is not realistic. Nevertheless, "mistakes" should not be carried one more day after they are detected, and this time must be as short as possible. My advice to managers: don't wait for a year before you review new employees; do a review within 30 and 60 days. By identifying and discussing weaknesses early, you have a better chance of correcting them before they become large negatives.

There is a saying that goes *"small business owners are too quick to hire and to slow to fire"*. How true this is! I hope I don't appear heartless by making this statement, but it is fact that we tend to "carry dead wood" far too long. Why do we do it? The answer is as simple as it is wrong. When we need somebody we need them NOW and we tend to rush the process to cover the pressing need. However, when we know we need to fire someone we tend to delay the action because "we don't have anybody else to do that job", or because we feel sorry for the person getting fired.

Are we doing the business good by these actions? Of course not; small businesses cannot afford the luxury of keeping someone just because we don't have anybody else to do his or her job, or to be magnanimous by keeping a less-than-efficient employee because we feel sorry for that person.

It is also unfair to the employee because most likely, he or she is in the wrong job and at a dead-end in the company as a low performer. Releasing the person would give him/her an opportunity to get into a better situation and have a better future. Additionally, assuming that a bad performer received a review as such, how can a manager justify keeping him/her?

Of course, not all mistakes need to be permanent. Some people take longer to develop into a job but they can be very valuable once they reach the level of competence required. In these cases, it is the manager's responsibility to train and develop new (and all) employees and to give them the opportunity to reach the target level.

What is the alternative that I propose? How about daily reviews? No, I don't mean daily formal reviews to compound the problems described above! I always told my employees (of any level) that they are being reviewed daily by our continuous interaction.

## Pro-performance reviews

Wikipedia definition of performance reviews further includes: "It is the process of obtaining, analyzing, and recording information about the relative worth of an employee to the organization."

Do performance reviews really determine the true worth of an employee? Do they accurately evaluate the ways in which an employee has contributed? Do employees participate in the evaluation or is it a "one-way" edict? Are they applied in the development of the employee or are they insignificant pieces of paper that when the review has been read and filed away, don't really mean anything to the employee or the organization?

Those in the "pro-performance review" camp say that they are necessary for companies' success and still continue the practice. People can always improve on something and performance reviews are a huge dose of reality and if employees take advantage of that dose they can improve their performance.

When performance reviews are done right, managers are able to evaluate where an employee is on his or her career path and his or her strengths and weakness and what they need to do to improve and become more successful. This success, in turn, benefits the company as a whole.

This debate raises many questions such as: How can we make performance reviews more productive and less distasteful? The answer to this is to make its objectives very clear to all involved and making the employees active participants and not just the recipients of whatever management wants to transmit. Managers should invest time in continuous communication regarding performance of each individual and in coaching in real time.

Continuous feedback is the solution to prevent a major danger of performance reviews; i.e., they should not be a surprise, but rather they should be part of a continuous loop of planning, coaching and providing spontaneous feedback.

While emphasis is placed on looking backward to judge performance, at least equal emphasis must be placed on how to improve future performance and in developing the organization. I also believe that performance reviews should be disengaged from the determination of compensation to the extent that performance review time should not be expected by employees to be "pay increase time".

© 2000 Randy Glasbergen.  www.glasbergen.com

"My performance review says I have trouble accepting responsibility. Is that MY fault?!"

## PART II – Other Methods

There are various alternatives suggested in the literature ranging from the most popular "get rid of performance reviews" to variations that make changes to the process. Culbert, for example, suggests performance *previews* rather than reviews, and he defines them as "discussions that take place when there is still time to get good results".

Regardless of alternatives chosen meetings between employees and bosses are necessary to determine what they need from each other to get the desired results for company and employee.

Some companies use a system by which managers of each department meet to discuss the strengths and weaknesses of their employees and to approve promotions or penalties and even dismissals of employees. Needless is to say employees do not like this process and even the managers are not sure what are the objectives to reach with this method.

Does the company benefit? Does the employee benefit? It seems that this method is less about employees' actual contribution and more about managerial opinions about the employees' leadership skills and growth potential; in other words, it does not reward performance but judges people on non-measurable issues.

When the real purpose of performance reviews is not clear it compounds the pain of conducting the reviews. Not knowing whether they are intended primarily to benefit the organization or the individual pins a huge question mark on the process; why do them when their purpose is unknown or not clear?

Ideally the purpose of reviews should be to drive the organization towards successful performance and to ensure that the work of employees directly contribute to the goals of the organization as well as the development of the employees. Therefore it may be better to refer to performance reviews as "personal development reviews" while maintaining the organizational objectives.

Almost any system would work if organizations truly fostered an environment of continuous feedback, and that's why I submit my proposal of frequent and constant reviews.

## Ranking of employees

Another approach to evaluation of organizations is ranking of its employees from top to bottom. Many companies implement this system and inevitably some employees get high marks while others are ranked as below average or worst. This means that even in an organization of high performers many will receive a rating that will not make them happy, and in an average team where no one is working to expectations, someone is going to look like a star.

This method eliminates the weak management option of grading everyone as "above average" or "superior" or similar flattering descriptions; instead they foster a lot of unhealthy competition among peers. Nobody wants to be in the bottom group and would do what they must to avoid it, even if it includes making someone else look bad. It can also be an unfair method if it is used to arbitrarily eliminate certain portion of employees.

In Microsoft's "stack racking" method for example, the system grades employees on a curve, resulting in a certain number of participants that must be labeled underperformers. This kind of ranking creates a sense of helplessness and failure and encourages people to backstab their co-workers, and can also fictitiously enhance someone's standing. I have also observed cases where a manager uses biased ranking to benefit certain individuals who are his or her favorites.

Interestingly, in an article of December 2, 2013 Jack Welch [7] severely critiqued what is generally called "rank and yank" system of ranking employees. I say interestingly because it was Jack Welsh who as CEO of General Electric implemented the system, or at least that's how his system was interpreted. He—as he described repeatedly in his books and articles—applied the 20-70-10 rule in which the bottom 10% had to be weeded out and management needed to concentrate on the other 90%. To be fair, he was not a proponent of quick dismissal for the "bottom 10%"—as he explains in the December article— but rather to first try to find them the right job, and if this is not possible then show them the door.

Critics of this system claim that it encourages employees to practice tactics of damaging others in order to improve their position. It is also unfair in that those at the bottom are not necessarily there for their own fault as perhaps they may not have received the proper training and/or attention. Jack prefers to call the system "differentiation" and he defines it as a way for every employee to know where he or she stands, and this is achieved by performance appraisals and in this they also apply the 20-70-10 rule or a similar one.

It is not surprising then that rating people on a numerical scale isn't a popular practice. A 1997 national survey by the Society for Human Resource Management found that only 5 percent of employees were satisfied with their companies' review process. Proponents of forced ranking claim that it is more effective than qualitative systems for employee appraisal in which employees don't receive frank or honest appraisals because managers are not capable to give them, for whatever reason.

They claim that ranking eliminates surprises and even lawsuits, when poorly-performing employees are dismissed. Opponents on the other hand, claim that it hurts teamwork and innovation. I believe that at best forced ranking systems may produce a short-term improvement in performance that soon levels out, likely because the worst performers are weeded out.

In a *Businessweek* article, Jeffrey Pfeffer [8], a professor at Stanford University's Graduate School of Business notes that "peer comparisons invariably create competition and discourage collaboration". This competition can make people unwilling to share knowledge or to cooperate with others, thus reducing the value to an organization. This method also requires that half the staff be rated below average, creating a threat to people's self-esteem as nobody likes to be "below average" and most people would resist this label.

## 360-degrees reviews

Advocates of non-traditional performance reviews suggest 360-degree feedback; a process also known as multi-rater feedback, multi-source feedback, or multi-source assessment by which feedback comes from members of an employee's immediate work circle whereby individuals are reviewed not just by their bosses, but by their subordinates, peers and it may also include a self-evaluation. It can also include feedback from external sources, such as customers and suppliers or other stakeholders. The feedback is often anonymous.

When used properly it is a positive addition to performance management systems. The purpose of the 360 degree feedback is to assist each individual to understand his or her strengths and weaknesses, and how he/she is perceived by others. It aims to contribute insights into aspects of his or her work needing professional development.

The results from a 360-degree evaluation can be used by the person receiving the feedback to plan and map specific paths in their development, or by the organization to evaluate itself and the "climate" within it. Results are also used by some organizations in making administrative decisions related to pay and promotions and even about changes in the structure of the organization.

## History of 360-degree feedback

One of the earliest recorded uses of surveys to gather information is about the German military to evaluate performance of its soldiers during WW II. The first reported use of information from multiple sources about employees refers to the 1950s at Esso Research and Engineering Company. The idea of 360-degree feedback gained momentum and by the 1990s most companies embraced the concept. However, collecting and analyzing the data collected had to be done by hand on paper requiring complex manual calculations and much time consuming.

Currently, thanks to the ubiquity of the Internet and the ability to conduct evaluations online, 360-degree feedback use steadily increased in popularity. Lately, Internet-based surveys and analysis have become standard in corporate development using a growing menu of useful features.

## Advantages and caveats

A well-developed and planned system, implemented with care and thorough training can be a very powerful and useful tool to evaluate people and organizations and to plan their development. However, just doing 360-degree reviews because "it's the thing to do" or because "everyone else is doing it" can be detrimental to the organization and even hurtful to some people.

It is a tool that can provide employees the opportunity to receive valuable performance feedback from supervisor, peers and subordinates and the information can be used both to plan individual development and team work. It also allows each individual to understand how his performance as an employee, coworker, or staff member is viewed by others, providing a mirror to compare individual self-evaluation with the perception of others. This can be a reaffirmation of self-value or a wakeup call into the reality of his/her value to the organization.

The system can be used to provide information about one or more individuals (all raters provide information about one person) or to execute a true 360-degrees where each rater evaluates every other participant (all participants evaluate each other). One negative to be aware of is that peer reviews tend to be too lenient.

Caution should be exercised to prevent potential negative effects of its use. Firstly, raters should be people that are familiar with the performance and interaction of those being evaluated (whether is one person or each other). Impartiality is essential and thus preconceived feelings about some participant (either positive or negative) must be avoided.

Personal affronts or comments not related to the purpose of the evaluation can convert the tool into an organization killer. Similarly, providing negative feedback about someone only to help one's cause, or embellishing someone's evaluation to "help a friend" can cause much damage to the organization and to individuals.

In my experience of using 360-degrees evaluations multiple times in various organizations, the first time it is used is the most difficult because people are learning for the first time what others think of them, and this experience can be an "ego-killer". Successive use of the tool (I suggest yearly use) are more pleasant as people understand that the evaluations are intended to help and not to hurt. How the information collected is used is also critical.

I have used 360 degrees reviews among CEOs of small and midsize companies who participated in peer advisory boards. In these exercises, every member reviewed all other members. It was extremely interesting to see not only the reaction of the members to learn what perception others had of their traits, but also how much they learned from the exercise and how appreciative all of them were for the lessons learned. I should note too that we had to go through a period of "learning" that the inputs were given in good faith and only with the purpose of helping.

## Other methods

There are other methods used by some people but most—if not all—are variations of those listed. One that perhaps is somewhat different is the behavioral anchored rating scale (BARS). It emphasizes how behaviors, traits and skills reflect on performance. It provides specific standards for job performance and thus it must be updated when job requirements change.

Another method is the critical incidents review process. It focuses on critical behaviors that are necessary to perform a job. It requires the development of the crtical list and it evaluates critical incidents of behavior. A plus of it is that it links employee behavior with job performance, but on the negative side it depends on a clear definition of the critical behaviors, and this is not always easy to identify for each job. Training managers on how to evaluate behavioral characteristics is crucial and not easy.

I have also seen Mamagement By Objectives methods applied in various forms, but they are mostly a result of a bad or wrog interpretation of the true MBO process.

# PART III - My Proposed Alternative

So, what are the alternatives? Should we skip reviews altogether? Should reviews be outlawed as negative experiences that do nothing to improve performance and provide fair and just rewards? Not completely. I favor a different approach. One that proved to yield excellent results for me during my extensive management career.

Did I scrap the formal reviews altogether? No, but I used them to define mutually agreed to goals and objectives for the employee to which they will be measured. What does this mean? That I used a "management by objectives method (MBO)" and subsequent reviews by the same method which I label RBGO (reviews by goals and objectives).

Obviously the MBO is not a new system or management fad; to the contrary, it has been around forever (it seems). It was first outlined by Peter Drucker in 1954 in his book *"The Practice of Management"* [9]. The system is used sporadically but many times it isn't well understood or used.

## What is MBO?

Wikipedia: "Management by objectives (MBO), or Management by Goals and Objectives (MBGO), also known as management by results (MBR), is a process of defining objectives within an organization so that management and employees agree to the objectives and understand what they need to do in the organization in order to achieve them".

MBO is a process of agreeing upon objectives within an organization so that management and employees agree to the objectives and understand what they are in the organization. It is a systematic and organized approach that allows management to focus on achievable goals and to attain the best possible results from available resources.

MBO aims to increase the overall performance of an organization by aligning goals and objectives throughout the organization. The essence of MBO is participative goal setting because management and employees jointly participate in setting the goals, choosing the course of actions and decision making to reach those goals.

An important part of the MBO is the measurement and the comparison of the employee's actual performance with the standards set. Ideally, when employees themselves have been involved with the goal setting and choosing the course of action to be followed by them, they are more likely to fulfill their responsibilities.

The principle behind Management by Objectives (MBO) is to create empowered employees who have clarity of the roles and responsibilities expected from them, understand their objectives to be achieved and thus help in the achievement of organizational as well as personal goals. Empowerment creates motivation; Involving employees in the whole process of goal setting increases employee job satisfaction and commitment.

A prerequisite of this system is that the personal objectives have to be in line with the company's objectives. The system aims to improve performance by matching the goals of the company with the individual and departmental goals and objectives of the entire organization.

MBO received a boost when it was declared to be an integral part of "The HP Way", the widely acclaimed management style of Hewlett-Packard, a computer company. At every level within Hewlett-Packard, managers had to develop objectives and integrate them with those of other managers and of the company as a whole. This was done by producing written plans showing what people needed to achieve if they were to reach those objectives. The plans were then shared with others in the corporation and coordinated.

The goals and objectives set for all employees must originate and be corresponding to the strategic plan of the company or the department. A well developed and functional strategic plan must be the origin of the goals set for all employees. The strategic plan must be effectively communicated throughout the company and must let all employees know how their roles and performance against goals will impact the success of the company and their participation in it.

Employees get strong input from management (acting as mentors) to identify their objectives, time lines for completion, reviews targets and definition of completion of the goals. The process must include ongoing tracking and feedback to reach objectives. Performance reviews based on this management method should then be called RBO or RBG&O (Reviews By Goals and Objectives).

## Advantages

What is the difference between RBO and the standard review method? RBO eliminates the objectivity of performance judgment; i.e., it does not depend on the difficult impartiality of a manager over multiple employees. With the RBO method—when used properly—there is no subjectivity, no favoritisms or personal dislikes; results are clear, the goals were met or they were not, there is no ambiguity.

In a RBO process a manager still meets "formally" with the employee but they meet to review progress achieved on the goals previously set. Judgment then is easy; were the goals met? Were they met on time? How many did not reach completion and why? Did performance exceed the goals set? Did the employee achieve extra merits?

The same meeting is also used to develop and set new goals for the new period. These goals must be jointly developed and agreed to—rather than being dictated by the manager—to ensure buy-in of the employee and to prevent future discrepancies. The frequency of these meetings depends on the length of the goals, but always ensuring that there are periodic ongoing progress reviews. Managers must not wait until the target date for completion to see if the goals will be met or not.

Reviewing progress close to the target date would be too late if the task or project is behind schedule; it would not provide an opportunity for the manager to coach the employee to catch up or to provide the help that the employee may need.

Another benefit of the RBO process is that, contrary to the traditional method, all parties benefit from it. The employee learns and improves because the manager guides him/her through the goals set and, hopefully, teaches the employee to accomplish them. Also, the employee knows exactly how he/she is being measured and what is required of him/her.

The manager benefits because he/she has employees that respond to the guidance and become more productive and efficient, and the company benefits from the increased productivity generated by happier employees and managers.

I've heard people claim that the RBO process cannot be used for production line workers or other low level employees because it is not practical to set goals for them. This is a fallacy as goals can be easily developed, monitored and measured for employees of any level.

A fairly recent article whose author I don't remember, discussed the MBO system and related theories of Peter Drucker and Paul Deming. The article included supporters as well as detractors of MBO. I found it interesting that most of the detractors were executives or employees of large companies. In fact, Deming also disagreed with Drucker but later in life Drucker claimed that if MBO fails it would be because it was not implemented correctly. I can understand the difficulties of integrating in a large company all the different hierarchical levels into common objectives, but this should not be a problem at the group or department level.

For all these reasons I favor scrapping the traditional employee performance reviews and adopting a Management by Objectives (MBO) and Review By Objectives (RBO) process that ensures value of the process, fairness in performance judgment (measurement), and eliminates all the negative consequences of the traditional process.

## Unique features of the MBO process

Behind the principle of Management by Objectives (MBO) is for employees to have a clear understanding of the roles and responsibilities expected of them. They can understand how their activities relate to the achievement of the organization's goal and thus it can be a source of pride and motivation. It also places importance on fulfilling the personal goals of each employee.

Some of the important features and advantages of MBO are:

1. Motivation – Involving employees in the whole process of goal setting and increasing employee empowerment. This increases employee job satisfaction and commitment.
2. Better communication and coordination – Frequent reviews and interactions between superiors and subordinates helps to maintain harmonious relationships within the organization and helps to solve many problems caused by faulty communications or misinterpretations.

3. Clarity of goals and the purpose of each goal and its effect on the organization.
4. Subordinates tend to have a higher commitment to objectives they set for themselves than for those imposed on them by another person.
5. Managers can ensure that objectives of the subordinates are linked to the organization's objectives.

Goals and standards are set for the next defined period and include scheduled reviews and continued feedback. The goals set must be clear and in full agreement between the parties. This doesn't mean that the employees are the drivers of the goals, but they must buy into the reasons and expected outcome of the goals proposed by management and set as priorities. There must be a strong linkage between organizational goals and performance targets of the employees.

Of course goals are derived from the objectives of the company and of the department or group. Thus, some objectives may be collective for a department or for the whole company while others can be individualized. In either case they must be quantified and monitored using reliable management information systems in an objective way.

"Millennials" (those born between the late 1970s and early 1990s) are accustomed to constant and instant feedback and they want and expect the same at work from their employers. Many jobs are heavily project-oriented and while reviews are often done at the completion of the project, it is much more productive to provide ongoing reviews to ensure the project is progressing satisfactorily. It's hard for someone to get better at something if he/she receives feedback on performance just once a year.

Bill Packard, one of the two founders of Hewlett-Packard, said of MBO:
"No operating policy has contributed more to Hewlett-Packard's success … MBO … is the antithesis of management by control. The latter refers to a tightly controlled system of management of the military type … Management by objectives, on the other hand, refers to a system in which overall objectives are clearly stated and agreed upon, and which gives people the flexibility to work toward those goals in ways they determine best for their own areas of responsibility".

## Limitations

I recognize that there are some possible limitations to the impact of managing by objectives and care should be taken to avoid them. For example, setting goals and managing by monitoring progress on those goals should not be substitutes for using a carefully developed plan as a driver of outcomes. The environment, resources and "culture" prevalent in the organization can play a role in the setting and achievement of goals and thus they must be considered in judging the completion of goals. Also, setting arbitrary goals can hamper the ability to improve dramatically–or drive the wrong improvement behaviors entirely.

The use of MBO and RBO needs to be carefully aligned with the culture of the organization. Employees must be rated on the completion of goals and their contributions to the organization, but not judged against an ideal employee.

Reviews should address the importance of successfully avoiding obstacles and limitations as essential to reaching a goal. Obstacles such as lacking adequate resources, planning methodology, informational tools and even perceived management support must be taken into account both in setting the goals and in reviewing progress against them.

MBO can play a key role in management today but rather than set objectives from a cascade process, objectives should be discussed and agreed to by all parties, based upon a strategic picture being available to employees. Engagement of employees in the objective setting process is a strategic prerequisite.

"What gets measured gets done" is a well-used maxim of performance measurement and it is true in that measuring performance frequently one assures that tasks get done and get done as they are supposed to. However, in most organizations employee performance is evaluated and not measured. True, criteria such as loyalty, attitude, "team playing" and perhaps others are not measurable in the true sense of the word, but their impact on performance can be measured at least indirectly.

Rating performance can be quite subjective for the criteria mentioned and for others particularly in the service sector, but measurements can be applied in most instances. It may be difficult to define measurements for some professions, but careful consideration of job demands and attributes can make it doable. A surgeon for example, can be measured on the number of operations performed on a given day with ample success and with the commendation of the patient and support staff.

## Potential for misuse

The potential for misuse of the MBO process is always latent, particularly by those who don't understand the process or those who try to take advantage of it for personal gains. If the boss puts pressure on employees to produce results but without the necessary two-way communication, the process will not result in the benefits desired. The boss maybe looking to achieve his/her goals without concern for the damage induced in the employee. Rather than allowing for dialogue and growth they allow the program to become a session for criticism and "tongue-lashing".

Another fallacy is for managers to see MBO as a total system that can handle all management problems. This can lead to forcing issues on the system that is not intended to handle, thus eliminating the effects it should have on performance and coaching.

Some of the criticism of MBO includes the argument that it takes a few years to be effective. This is really without foundation as it can be very easy to implement; however, training of management and employees is mandatory for its success. Some detractors claim that it requires too much paperwork, when in reality it can eliminate the unpopular forms needed for traditional reviews.

Some claim difficulty in measuring key operations. There may be some truth to this in very special cases, but measurements don't need to be complicated and the simplest they are, the better the results will be. Perhaps because of this claim there are also opinions that because of faults in the MBO process appraisals are sometimes made on personality traits rather than on performance.

Another negative comment is that it is not easy to set measurable objectives for staff groups who only exist to help the operational groups achieve their objectives. However, as I claim elsewhere in this book, measurements can be developed and applied easily to any job classification.

Care must be taken not to sacrifice organizational goals in favor of personal or group objectives. For example, reducing travel expenses at the expense of increased corporate sales. If this occurs, it surely would be due to poor management. Similarly, employees my not wish to be responsible for goals forced upon them if they may lead to ill-feelings among other employees.

The main cause of failures of the process if they occur is likely due to poor training or poor management acumen.

**Managerial focus**

According to Drucker managers should "avoid the activity trap", getting so involved in their day to day activities that they forget their main purpose or objective. Managers should participate in the strategic planning process, and implement those performance systems, designed to help the organization perform as expected.

The MBO process is about setting objectives and then breaking these down into more specific goals or key results. Consequently, in the MBO process, managers focus on the result achieved, not on the activity and in a good system they must empower and delegate to others and act as coaches to guide subordinates and ensure the accurate completion of tasks.

The system should get managers and empowered employees acting in unison to implement and achieve their individual plans, which automatically achieve those of the organization. To achieve this management must make sure that the system allows for everybody within the organization to have a clear understanding of the objectives of that organization and comprehensive awareness of their personal roles and responsibilities in achieving those aims.

## Where to use MBO

Contrary to some opinions I believe that the MBO process can be used in most—if not all—situations, with some adjustments. For example, some people say that it cannot be used at the lowest levels of an organization, but I disagree. Measurements can be applied to any job and any task and thus, performance of any job can be measured by the goals reached.

For example, line operators obviously can be measured in parts-per-period made and other parameters can also be added, such as quality of the parts, equipment utilization, etc. Janitorial employees can be measured in productivity and quality; sales personnel can be measured not just in sales volumes but also in number of contacts made, success of those contacts, referrals obtained, and many other parameters. Essentially, measurements are only limited by the imagination of management and their applicability to tasks at hand.

## Setting goals

Wikipedia: "A goal is a desired result a person or a system envisions, plans and commits to achieve a personal or organizational desired end-point in some sort of assumed development. Many people endeavor to reach goals within a finite time by setting deadlines."

It is roughly similar to purpose or aim, the anticipated result which guides reaction, or an end, which is an object, either a physical object or an abstract object, that has intrinsic value.

The major outcome of strategic planning is the setting of the objectives and goals for the organization based on the vision of the owner (in small businesses) and the vision and mission statement of the company. A goal is an aim to reach an objective in a specific period that can be short or long. In the case of long-period goals intermediate goals should be set.

Long-range goals are set through strategic planning and are translated into activities that will ensure reaching the goal through operational planning. Those activities include strategies, action plans and resources utilization plans.

## Setting objectives

Setting objectives involves a continuous process of evaluating strengths and weaknesses of the business and of decision-making regarding where the business is going. For individual and group objectives knowledge of the individuals and of the unit is a vital starting point. Well defined objectives must be focused on results, not on activities.

Strategic planning is done at the highest levels with other managers or key players also involved; group or departmental planning is also done and includes operational planning. The first step in operational planning is defining the result expected by the end of the designated cycle. Action plans for each goal are developed specifying responsible parties, resources needed and other pertinent details.

Management need to apply a feedback analysis to compare actual results with expectations. Must review results at regular intervals, and compare them with the expectations previously determined. When taking an action, one must determine what is expected to happen. Using the feedback analysis as a guide strengths must be reinforced and a plan developed to eliminate weaknesses and then determine what the next round of objectives will be.

Communicate, communicate, communicate; employees and managers must be on the "same page" regarding goals, what constitutes achievement, what management expects, what the rules are, what needs improvement and what the rewards and penalties are. Managers must also share why the employee's job is important and how it can benefit or hurt the company.

Since the individual goals should be based on the strategic plan of the company and/or the department, employees must be knowledgeable of and hopefully participate in its development.

Coaching must include not just how to complete the goals, but also what employees can do to improve their performance. Likely there will be disagreements and they must be cleared immediately; allowing a difference of opinion to foster can develop into a more serious issue. Building trust is essential to team work and team success. Encourage participation and new ideas; this can go a long way in motivating employees.

In order to set goals the expectations needed to achieve them must be clearly communicated and understood, but they must also be accepted by all. Depending on the size of the project and the length of the goals, manager and team must work together to set interim goals with their own expectations. Review dates for these goals must be set and those dates must be kept by both manager and employee. Skipping review dates by managers would transmit a perception that these reviews—and therefore the tasks—are not important.

Employees need to know what they're doing that can be improved—but also what they're doing that is good. Everyone likes praise and receiving it is a great motivator. I always used the maxim "catch them doing something right" as an opportunity to praise employees. Employees need to know that their employer is on their side; that they can count on management support. Use as an aphorism that a mistake is an opportunity to learn and apply it regularly. Do not allow the perception that mistakes are opportunities for psychological mugging as reprisal.

Once expectations, goals and reviews are set, delegate, empower and ... get out of the way! Knowing how to delegate is imperative to good relations and success of the team. *(See my E-book "Delegate to Succeed", SkillBites.net [10])*. A good manager must be available as counselor and mentor guiding employees to reach the goals. Be careful too of "up delegation".

Another important factor to the success of the goals and good relations is to eliminate unnecessary or unproductive tasks that take away from the efficient performance towards the tasks on hand. Eliminating burdensome tasks that work against the goals of the project will be seen by employees as providing support by management and will respond by working better and smarter themselves.

Allow me to reiterate, for your employees to be passionate about their work and be looking to improve their performance, they must be involved in the development of the goals and objectives. Setting goals should not be an edict or a dictatorial process; goals should be the result of productive discussion between manager and employee in a way that accomplishes the objectives of the company or department while at the same time lifting the employee's motivation because he/she is an active participant of the decisions.

Listen compassionately, involve employees in decision making, offer positive feedback, be fair and reward work well done, and witness employees' passion for work grow to higher levels.

## Final comments

The value of MBO is demonstrated in a 1991 comprehensive review by Robert Rodgers and John Hunter of thirty years of research on the impact of Management by Objectives; they concluded that companies whose CEOs demonstrated high commitment to MBO showed, on average, a 56% gain in productivity. Companies with CEOs who showed low commitment only saw a 6% gain in productivity.

My advice then to the powers to be, is to scrap the traditional employee performance reviews and adopt a Management by Objectives (MBO) and RBO process that ensures value of the process, fairness in performance judgment, and eliminates all the negative consequences of the traditional process.

Incidentally, another erroneous practice is to tie-in performance reviews with salary increases. Creating this practice aggravates all the negatives of the traditional reviews and also of the MBO program because employees feel inevitably entitled to an increase at "review time". I much favor a disengagement of the two, associating increases only to the achievement of goals as jointly developed.

"Review time", whether by traditional reviews or any other process, becomes a desirable date for employees but for the wrong reason. When the review takes place it can be a happy occasion or the source for unhappiness and even confrontations. Nevertheless, to change this practice it will be necessary to educate everyone on the "new system" but also to ensure a fair implementation with fair salary adjustments.

## Tips to prevent litigation

One of the critical aspects of performance appraisals—whether by "standard" reviews or MBO—is the risk of litigation by disgruntled employees. Therefore, the company must have and adhere to a process that ensures fair, consistent and legally sound appraisal systems. To this end make sure the system complies with the following:

- Communicate to all employees the performance standards that the company will maintain. The job description for each position must clearly define the performance expected, including rewards and penalties resulting from it. The job description should be accepted as a contract between the employee and the company, and as such it should determine the actions resulting from its compliance.

- If there is a problem with an unproductive employee don't wait until "review time" to act. If a manager tolerates an employee with a performance problem and then give the employee a negative assessment—or worse yet, a termination—the employee can claim that the action was discriminatory and may be able to show that no opportunity for improvement was given.

- Managers and supervisors should be trained on the right way to evaluate and communicate employee performance and in the effective compliance with the company evaluation policies.
- Ensure that employees are properly informed and given prompt and relevant feedback. Evaluations that are vague, subjective or inappropriate may lead to litigation. Moreover, give the employee plenty of opportunity to challenge or at least comment on the evaluation; this will support your claim that acted properly.
- Document, document, document all evaluations and performance problems religiously and on standard company policy forms and provide the employee with a copy of the document. Have the employee acknowledge receipt of it.

To ensure an effective, legally sound appraisal include the following:

- Implementation of a good job description as a contract between employee and company. The job description must be based on a job analysis that describes duties and responsibilities necessary for the job to be performed successfully. As covered above, it must include performance standards as well as expectations and rewards and penalties[11].
- Ensure that the system is designed so that all managers and supervisors implement it fairly

and consistently. Company standard procedures must include directions to check if the system is implemented as designed.

- Evaluation forms must become part of the standard operating procedure (SOP) of the company and must be well understood by all managers and employees.
- Make sure that the performance being measured is clearly defined and correlates to the objectives that are critical to the success on the job.

There are many performance review checklist available online; I suggest using one as the basis for a company policy standard.

"I understand what you're trying to do here, Tom, but I'd appreciate it more if you'd actually do it."

# References:

(1) "Get Rid of Performance Reviews" by Samuel A. Culbert and Lawrence Rout, Copyright 2010.)

(2) "State of Performance Management"; A report by WorldatWork and Sibson Consulting, October 2010

(3) Kluger, A. N., & DeNisi, A. (1996). "The effects of feedback interventions on performance: A historical review, a meta-analysis, and a preliminary feedback intervention theory". *Psychological Bulletin*, 119(2), 254–284.

(4) "10Reasons to Get Rid of Performance Reviews", Samuel Culbert, The Huff post, February 13, 2014

(5) "Winning", Jack and Suzy Welch, Harper Business, 2004.

(6) "Performance Reviews Lose Steam,", Rachel Emma Silverman, The Wall Street Journal, Dec. 19, 2011

(7) "Rank and Junk?; That's Not How is Done"; Jack Welch, Linkedin, December 2, 2013

(8) "Low Grades For Performance Reviews"; Jeffrey Pfeffer, BusinessWeek, July 23, 2009.

(9) "The Practice of Management", Peter Drucker, 1954.

(10) "Delegate to Succeed", Oswald R. Viva; SkillBites, 2013.

(11) "The Essentials of a Complete Job Description" by Wayne Berry of Aquarius International, November 2007

# APPENDIX

## Goal setting *(using second person grammatical)*

Successful goal setting isn't as simple as wanting something. To have a goal is more than just wishful thinking; it's a process that has to be followed. Setting goals is more than deciding what you want to do. It involves figuring out what you need to do to get where you want to go and how long it will take you to get there.

Goals are set to meet defined objectives and the way in which you set them will affect how effective you will be in making them happen. Goals should be straightforward and emphasize what you want to accomplish.

Goals are the result of planning. When you go on a trip you have a destination as a goal but you also need the plan to get there (the route) and the methods (the driving) and action plans (what, where and how). If you don't have a plan in business, is like driving looking only at the rear view mirror; you know where you have been but you don't know where you are going.

Focus on Your Strengths. Successful goal setting means continually utilizing your strengths to get you ahead while keeping a secondary eye on the weaker parts of your game.

The first step to success is to know where you want to go. The second step is to have a plan to get there. Your goals are your road map. Follow them and you'll be well on your way.

Start with your long-term objectives. Next, establish short-term goals. These include monthly, weekly and even daily targets that will move you toward your long-term objectives.

Evaluate. Constantly strive to see what is working, and what is not. Don't restrain yourself from tweaking things that aren't working as well as you would like, and expand where you are doing things well.

Set a weekly or monthly reminder to go over your progress and readjust where necessary. Sometimes the difference between successful goal setting and failing is a simple tweak or two.

Be careful not to push yourself or your team too hard or too fast and be careful not to set yourself or your team up for failure. You have to stretch your talents and your company's resources to grow, but it's important to set reasonable goals.

Ensure the goals you set are very specific, clear and easy. Business goals must be in line with the strategic plan, and personal goals must be in line with the personal roadmap to achieve your plan.

Always use the S.M.A.R.T. model for setting goals.
- Specific
- Measurable
- Attainable
- Realistic & Responsible
- Timeline

## Specific

Goals should be straightforward and emphasize what you want to happen. Specifics help you to focus your efforts and clearly define what you are going to do.

Specific is the What, Why, and How of the SMART model.

- What are you going to do? Use action words such as direct, organize, coordinate, lead, develop, plan, build etc.
- Why is this important to do at this time? What do you want to ultimately accomplish?
- How are you going to do it? (By…)

Setting objectives is not sufficient; setting the right objectives is critical for effective performance management. Objectives such as obtain higher revenues or profits, increase shareholder value, superior customer satisfaction are marvelous but they don't tell anybody what to do and they fail to specify quantities, priorities and focus. They don't show the end goal and how to get there.

## Measurable

If you can't measure it, you can't manage it. In the broadest sense, the whole goal statement is a measure for the project; if the goal is accomplished, there is success. Short-term or small measurements should be built into the goal in order to monitor progress or make adjustments.

Choose a goal with measurable progress, so you can see the change occur. Establish concrete criteria for measuring progress toward the attainment of each goal you set. When you measure your progress, you stay on track, reach your target dates, and experience the exhilaration of achievement that spurs you on to continued effort required to reach your goals.

## Attainable

When you identify goals that are very important to you or to your business, you dedicate the effort to make them come true. You develop the attitudes, abilities, skills, and financial capacity to reach them. On the other hand, you probably won't commit to doing goals that are too far into the future or presently out of your reach. You may have the best of intentions, but knowing that it's a stretch for you, subconsciously you will stop giving it your best effort.

The feeling of success that you get by seeing progress in attaining a goal helps you to remain motivated.

## Realistic

This is not a synonym for "easy." Realistic, in this case, means doable. It means that the learning curve is not too steep; that you have the skills needed to do the work and that the project fits with the overall strategy and goals of the organization. A realistic project should push the skills and knowledge of the people working on it but it shouldn't break them.

Be sure to set goals that you can attain with some effort. If a goal is too difficult you may be setting yourself for failure, but if it's too easy it may send a message that you aren't very capable. Set the bar high enough for a satisfying achievement.

**Timely**

Set a timeframe for the goal. Putting an end point on your goal gives you a clear target to work towards. If you don't set a time, the commitment is too vague. It tends not to happen because you put it off in favor of "urgent" or perceivably more important things. Without a time limit, there's no urgency to start taking action.

Time too must be measurable, attainable and realistic.

**Goal setting as motivator**

Goal setting encourages participants to put in greater effort as they are driven to meeting them, and because managers are compelled to follow them, there is little chance of inadequate effort going unnoticed.

Goals focus attention towards goal-relevant activities and away from goal-irrelevant activities. They act as motivators; higher goals will induce greater effort while low goals induce lesser effort. However, if people are limited by constraints with regard to resources their work pace will suffer.

**Inspiring employees**

Getting people to accomplish something is much easier if they have the inspiration to do so. For employees to be inspired you need to be passionate about the business. If you as the leader project great enthusiasm for the business, you will generate a trickle-down effect in the organization. If you do not communicate excitement, how can you expect your people to get excited about it?

Your primary responsibility is to develop people and enable them to reach their full potential. Your people may come from diverse backgrounds, but they all have goals they want to accomplish. Create a "people environment" where they truly can be all they can be.

You will create that environment by having employees involved in the decision making process. If they are, they will participate much more enthusiastically than if you just give them orders. When given specific goals, employees tend to perform at a higher level. Telling them to do their best or giving no guidance increases ambiguity about what is expected and results in inferior performance. Employees need a set goal or model in order to perform at their best.

Don't make goals too easy or unimportant; increasing your employees' goal difficulty increases their challenges and enhances the amount of effort expended to achieve them. However, goals must be realistic. The more difficult goals lead to increased performance if they seem feasible, but if they seem too high, employees will give up when they fail to achieve them.

Listen to your employees and tell them you value their opinions, but you need to be sincere, not just give lip service. Prove it by incorporating their ideas when it makes sense to do so. Providing feedback enhances the effects of goal setting. Performance feedback keeps their behavior directed on the right target and encourages them to work harder to achieve the goal.

The enhancement of performance through goals requires feedback. Goal-setting may have little effect if individuals cannot check where the state of their performance is in relation to their goal. Let them know clearly and often how they are performing and how their performance affects (either positively or negatively) the performance of the company.

Do not wait to check on the progress of a project or task until a goal's target date is upon you because it will be too late to make corrections or to nudge the employee to improve progress. Instead, set firm periodic review dates when setting the goal and check on progress made and quality of the performance. This rule applies to all supervisors managing goals, from the CEO, to the lower line supervisor.

## Limitations

You must realize that goal-setting may have some limitations. In an organization, a goal of an employee may not align with the goals of the organization as a whole and they may even come into direct conflict with the goals of the company. It is critical then to assure that individual goals match the company's goals. Without aligning goals between the organization and the individual, performance may suffer.

Moreover, for complex tasks, goal-setting may actually impair performance. If an individual becomes more preoccupied with meeting the goals, rather than performing tasks, performance may suffer. These limitations are prevented by making sure that the goals follow the SMART definition.

## Setting goals effectively

In summary, answer the following questions when you are working on a strategic plan:
- Am I thinking the goals through and all aspects of them?
- What skills do I (the company) need to achieve them?
- What information & knowledge do I (the company) need?
- What help, assistance or collaboration do I (the company) need?
- What resources do I (the company) need?
- What can block progress?
- Am I (my team) making valid assumptions?
- Is there a better way of doing it?

## Some appropriate maxims

- The road to someday leads to the town of nowhere.
- Delete "someday" from your vocabulary; set firm dates for all your goals.

- "Insanity is doing the same things and expecting different results" (Albert Einstein)
- Invite and drive change in your organization; without change your company will not grow.
- "If you don't set goals you can't regret not reaching them" (Yogi Berra)
- Get in the habit of setting goals and putting in the effort to meet or exceed them.
- "If you set your goal low enough you will inevitably meet them" (O.R. Viva).
- Make your goals ambitious but realistic; you will feel a sense of accomplishment when you beat them.

Train your employees to set and manage goals. Regardless of their title or position they should be knowledgeable in the subject and should use goals on a regular basis. You may want to consider contracting a consultant to do the teaching.

# About the author:

Oswald R. Viva, CMC is President of V&A Management, LLC, of Acworth, GA, a management consulting firm dedicated to helping entrepreneurs and small companies achieve their potential. He is also an Executive Coach and Mentor, and a Certified Facilitator. In his long career as high-tech industry executive and consultant, Mr. Viva had multiple CEO and other "C" level positions, has participated in eight start-ups and has served on the Boards of seven entrepreneurial ventures. He is a former member of the Board of Directors of The Entrepreneurs Forum of Greater Philadelphia, he is a member of the Fortune Business Council. He can be reached by phone at 610-213-2903, or by email to oviva@vamanagementllc.com

www.ingramcontent.com/pod-product-compliance
Lightning Source LLC
Chambersburg PA
CBHW040838180526
45159CB00001B/230